1x 9/09
8/09 4/12

My Body

My Muscles

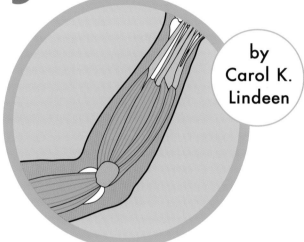

by
Carol K.
Lindeen

Consulting Editor: Gail Saunders-Smith, PhD

Consultant: James R. Hubbard, MD
Fellow in the American Academy of Pediatrics
Iowa Medical Society, West Des Moines, Iowa

Capstone
press®
Mankato, Minnesota®

Pebble Books are published by Capstone Press,
151 Good Counsel Drive, P.O. Box 669, Mankato, Minnesota 56002.
www.capstonepress.com

1 2 3 4 5 6 12 11 10 09 08 07

Library of Congress Cataloging-in-Publication Data
Lindeen, Carol, 1976–
    My muscles / by Carol K. Lindeen.
    p. cm.—(Pebble Books. My body)
    Summary: "Simple text and photographs describe muscles, what they do, and
how they work"—Provided by publisher.
    Includes bibliographical references and index.
    ISBN-13: 978-0-7368-6695-8 (hardcover)
    ISBN-10: 0-7368-6695-7 (hardcover)
    ISBN-13: 978-0-7368-7839-5 (softcover pbk.)
    ISBN-10: 0-7368-7839-4 (softcover pbk.)
    1. Muscles—Juvenile literature. I. Title. II. Series.
QP321.L63 2007
612.7'4—dc22   2006027843

Note to Parents and Teachers

The My Body set supports national science standards related to anatomy and the basic structure and function of the human body. This book describes and illustrates muscles. The photographs support early readers in understanding the text. The repetition of words and phrases helps early readers learn new words. This book also introduces early readers to subject-specific vocabulary words, which are defined in the Glossary section. Early readers may need assistance to read some words and to use the Table of Contents, Glossary, Read More, Internet Sites, and Index sections of the book.

Table of Contents

4

My Many Muscles

My muscles help me move.
I have muscles
in almost all parts
of my body.

My muscles
help me play.
I throw, skip, and jump.

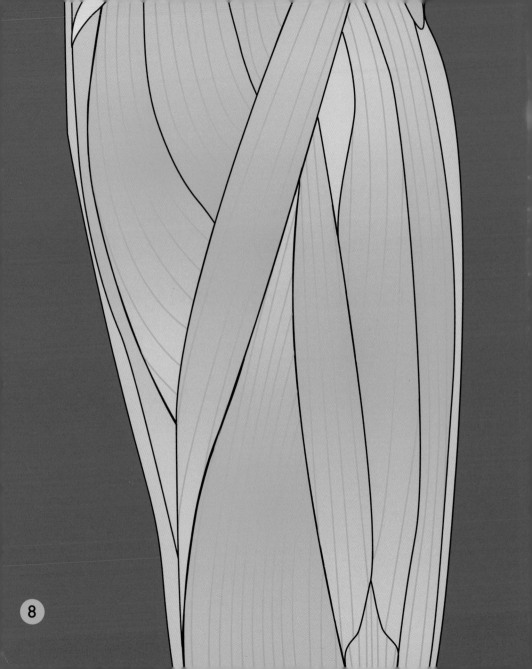

8

On the Inside

My muscles are bunches of tissues. The tissues stretch like rubber bands.

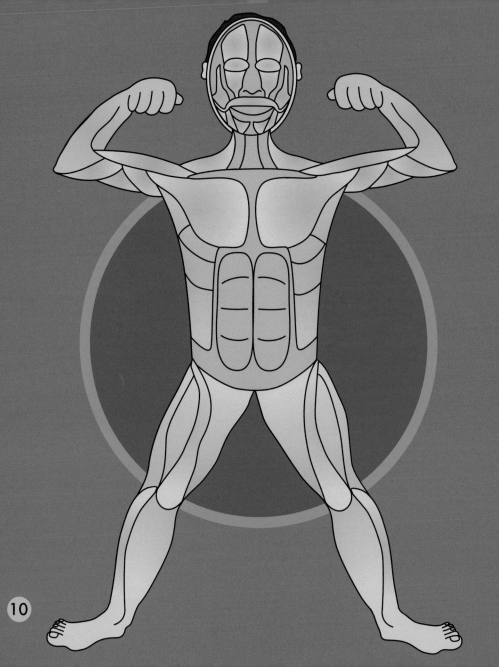

My muscles
are different shapes
and sizes.

My heart is a muscle.
It pumps blood through
my body.

My Muscles and My Body

My brain tells
my muscles
what to do.
My muscles
tighten and relax.

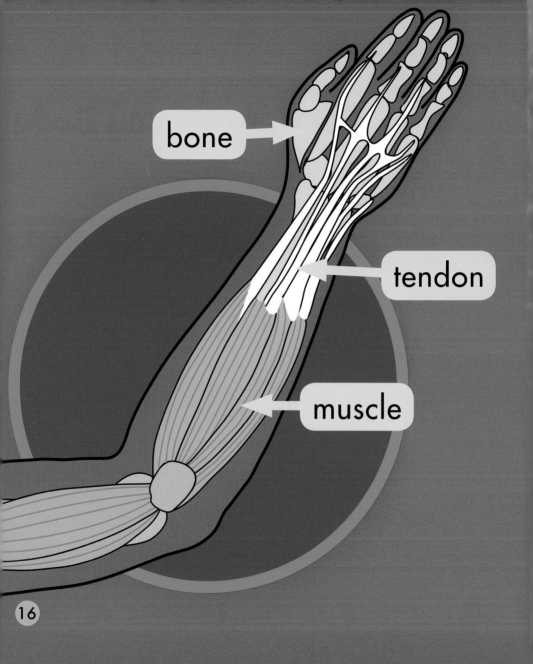

bone

tendon

muscle

Tendons join
my muscles
to my bones.

My muscles work together.
They pull my arms
up and down.

My muscles use energy
from the food I eat.
Being active keeps
my muscles strong.

Glossary

active—busy playing and exercising

relax—to loosen and lengthen

tendon—a strong cord of tissue that joins a muscle to a bone

tighten—to make something firm; muscles get shorter when they are tight.

tissue—a layer or bunch of soft, living material that makes up body parts; muscles and skin are made of tissue.

Read More

Fitzpatrick, Anne. *The Muscles*. The Human Body. North Mankato, Minn.: Smart Apple Media, 2003.

Ganeri, Anita. *Your Muscles and Bones*. How Your Body Works. Milwaukee: Gareth Stevens, 2003.

Internet Sites

FactHound offers a safe, fun way to find Internet sites related to this book. All of the sites on FactHound have been researched by our staff.

Here's how:

1. Visit *www.facthound.com*
2. Choose your grade level.
3. Type in this book ID **0736866957** for age-appropriate sites. You may also browse subjects by clicking on letters, or by clicking on pictures and words.
4. Click on the **Fetch It** button.

FactHound will fetch the best sites for you!

Index

Word Count: 101
Grade: 1
Early-Intervention Level: 14

Editorial Credits
Mari Schuh, editor; Bobbi J. Wyss, designer; Sandra D'Antonio, illustrator;
    Kelly Garvin, photo stylist

Photo Credits
Capstone Press/Karon Dubke, all